Africa

COLORING BOOK FOR KIDS!

DISCOVER THIS COLLECTION OF COLORING PAGES

Bold Illustrations
COLORING BOOKS

frica Africa Africa Africa

frica Africa Africa Africa

frica Africa Africa Africa

frica Africa Africa Africa

This is a Bleed Through Page If You Are Using a Colouring Marker or Pen!
Find Other Great Titles By searching for Bold Illustrations on Your Favorite Book Retailer
Amazon.Ca | Barnes & Noble (BN.Com) | Books A Million (BAM.Com)

frica Africa Africa Africa

frica Africa Africa Africa

frica Africa Africa Africa

frica Africa Africa Africa

frica Africa Africa Africa

frica Africa Africa Africa

This is a Bleed Through Page If You Are Using a Colouring Marker or Pen!
Find Other Great Titles By searching for Bold Illustrations on Your Favorite Book Retailer
Amazon.Ca | Barnes & Noble (BN.Com) | Books A Million (BAM.Com)

Bold Illustrations
COLORING BOOKS

frica Africa Africa Africa

frica Africa Africa Africa

frica Africa Africa Africa

Africa Africa Africa Africa

frica Africa Africa Africa

frica Africa Africa Africa
frica Africa Africa Africa

frica Africa Africa Africa

frica Africa Africa Africa

frica Africa Africa Africa

Africa Africa Africa Africa

frica Africa Africa Africa

frica Africa Africa Africa

frica Africa Africa Africa

This is a Bleed Through Page If You Are Using a Colouring Marker or Pen!

Find Other Great Titles By searching for Bold Illustrations on Your Favorite Book Retailer

Amazon.Ca | Barnes & Noble (BN.Com) | Books A Million (BAM.Com)

frica Africa Africa Africa

frica Africa Africa Africa

This is a Bleed Through Page If You Are Using a Colouring Marker or Pen!

Find Other Great Titles By searching for Bold Illustrations on Your Favorite Book Retailer

Amazon.Ca | Barnes & Noble (BN.Com) | Books A Million (BAM.Com)

Bold Illustrations

COLORING BOOKS

This is a Bleed Through Page If You Are Using a Colouring Marker or Pen!
Find Other Great Titles By searching for Bold Illustrations on Your Favorite Book Retailer
Amazon.Ca | Barnes & Noble (BN.Com) | Books A Million (BAM.Com)

Bold Illustrations
COLORING BOOKS

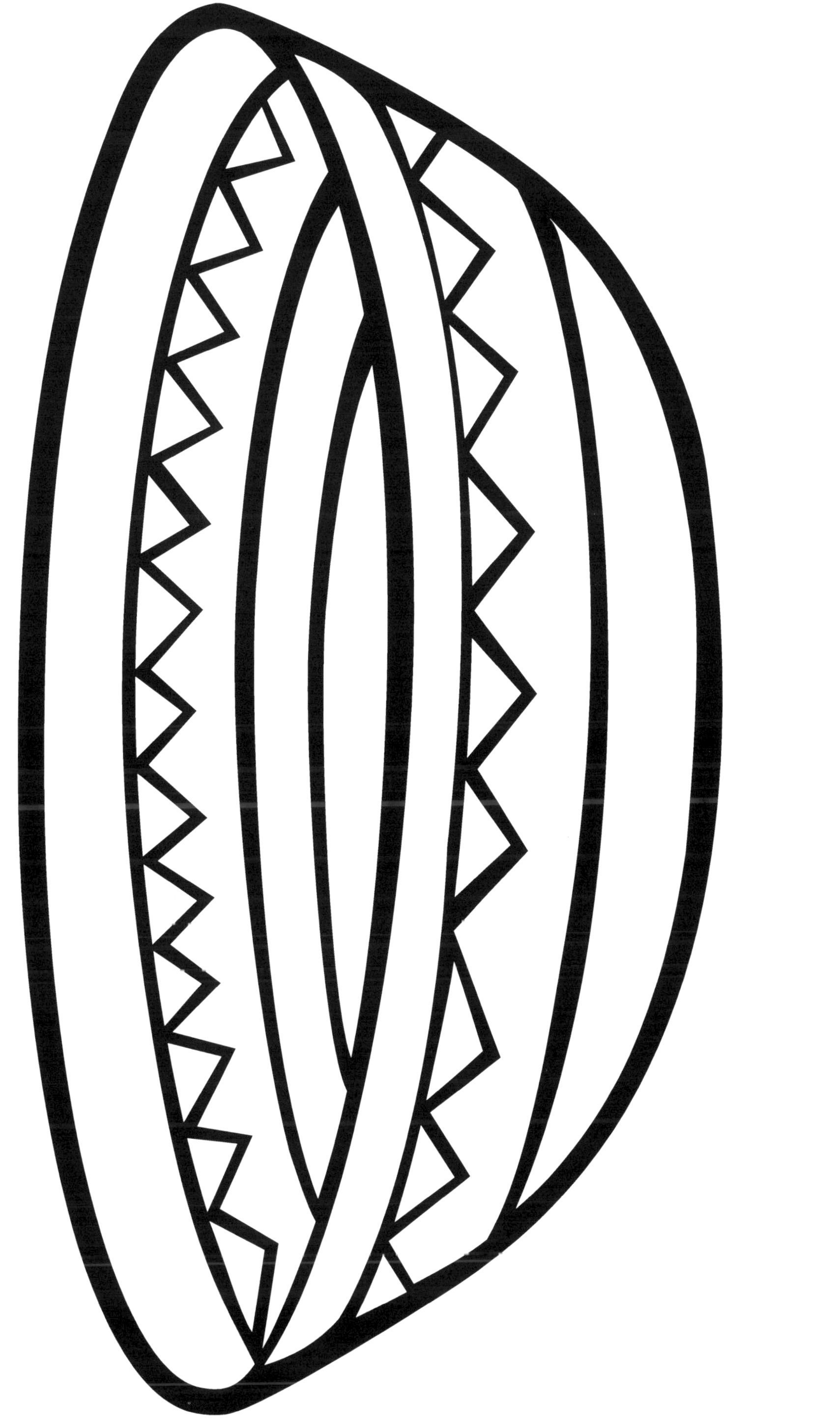

frica Africa Africa Africa

frica Africa Africa Africa

frica Africa Africa Africa
Africa Africa Africa Africa
frica Africa Africa Africa

This is a Bleed Through Page If You Are Using a Colouring Marker or Pen!
Find Other Great Titles By searching for Bold Illustrations on Your Favorite Book Retailer
Amazon.Ca | Barnes & Noble (BN.Com) | Books A Million (BAM.Com)

Bold Illustrations
COLORING BOOKS

frica Africa Africa Africa

Africa Africa Africa Africa

frica Africa Africa Africa

This is a Bleed Through Page If You Are Using a Colouring Marker or Pen!

Find Other Great Titles By searching for Bold Illustrations on Your Favorite Book Retailer

Amazon.Ca | Barnes & Noble (BN.Com) | Books A Million (BAM.Com)

frica Africa Africa Africa

frica Africa Africa Africa

frica Africa Africa Africa

Africa Africa Africa Africa Africa Africa

frica Africa Africa Africa

frica Africa Africa Africa

frica Africa Africa Africa

This is a Bleed Through Page If You Are Using a Colouring Marker or Pen!
Find Other Great Titles By searching for Bold Illustrations on Your Favorite Book Retailer
Amazon.Ca | Barnes & Noble (BN.Com) | Books A Million (BAM.Com)

Bold Illustrations
COLORING BOOKS

frica Africa Africa Africa

frica Africa Africa Africa

This is a Bleed Through Page If You Are Using a Colouring Marker or Pen!

Find Other Great Titles By searching for Bold Illustrations on Your Favorite Book Retailer

Amazon.Ca | Barnes & Noble (BN.Com) | Books A Million (BAM.Com)

frica Africa Africa Africa

Africa Africa Africa Africa

frica Africa Africa Africa

This is a Bleed Through Page If You Are Using a Colouring Marker or Pen!
Find Other Great Titles By searching for Bold Illustrations on Your Favorite Book Retailer
Amazon.Ca | Barnes & Noble (BN.Com) | Books A Million (BAM.Com)

Bold Illustrations
COLORING BOOKS

frica Africa Africa Africa

Africa Africa Africa Africa Africa Africa Africa Africa Africa

frica Africa Africa Africa

frica Africa Africa Africa

Africa Africa Africa

frica Africa Africa Africa

This is a Bleed Through Page If You Are Using a Colouring Marker or Pen!
Find Other Great Titles By searching for Bold Illustrations on Your Favorite Book Retailer
Amazon.Ca | Barnes & Noble (BN.Com) | Books A Million (BAM.Com)

Africa Africa Africa Africa
Africa Africa Africa Africa

This is a Bleed Through Page If You Are Using a Colouring Marker or Pen!

Find Other Great Titles By searching for Bold Illustrations on Your Favorite Book Retailer

Amazon.Ca | Barnes & Noble (BN.Com) | Books A Million (BAM.Com)

Bold Illustrations

COLORING BOOKS

frica Africa Africa Africa

frica Africa Africa Africa

This is a Bleed Through Page If You Are Using a Colouring Marker or Pen!
Find Other Great Titles By searching for Bold Illustrations on Your Favorite Book Retailer
Amazon.Ca | Barnes & Noble (BN.Com) | Books A Million (BAM.Com)

frica Africa Africa Africa

Africa Africa Africa Africa

frica Africa Africa Africa

This is a Bleed Through Page If You Are Using a Colouring Marker or Pen!
Find Other Great Titles By searching for Bold Illustrations on Your Favorite Book Retailer
Amazon.Ca | Barnes & Noble (BN.Com) | Books A Million (BAM.Com)

frica Africa Africa Africa

Africa Africa Africa Africa

frica Africa Africa Africa

This is a Bleed Through Page If You Are Using a Colouring Marker or Pen!
Find Other Great Titles By searching for Bold Illustrations on Your Favorite Book Retailer
Amazon.Ca | Barnes & Noble (BN.Com) | Books A Million (BAM.Com)

frica Africa Africa Africa

frica Africa Africa Africa

frica Africa Africa Africa

Africa Africa Africa Africa Africa

frica Africa Africa Africa

This is a Bleed Through Page If You Are Using a Colouring Marker or Pen!

Find Other Great Titles By searching for Bold Illustrations on Your Favorite Book Retailer

Amazon.Ca | Barnes & Noble (BN.Com) | Books A Million (BAM.Com)

frica Africa Africa Africa

frica Africa Africa Africa

frica Africa Africa Africa
Africa Africa Africa Africa
frica Africa Africa Africa

frica Africa Africa Africa
Africa Africa Africa Africa Africa Africa Africa
frica Africa Africa Africa

This is a Bleed Through Page If You Are Using a Colouring Marker or Pen!
Find Other Great Titles By searching for Bold Illustrations on Your Favorite Book Retailer
Amazon.Ca | Barnes & Noble (BN.Com) | Books A Million (BAM.Com)

frica Africa Africa Africa

Africa Africa Africa Africa

frica Africa Africa Africa

This is a Bleed Through Page If You Are Using a Colouring Marker or Pen!
Find Other Great Titles By searching for Bold Illustrations on Your Favorite Book Retailer
Amazon.Ca | Barnes & Noble (BN.Com) | Books A Million (BAM.Com)

Bold Illustrations
COLORING BOOKS

frica Africa Africa Africa

frica Africa Africa Africa

frica Africa Africa Africa

Africa Africa Africa Africa Africa

frica Africa Africa Africa

frica Africa Africa Africa

frica Africa Africa Africa

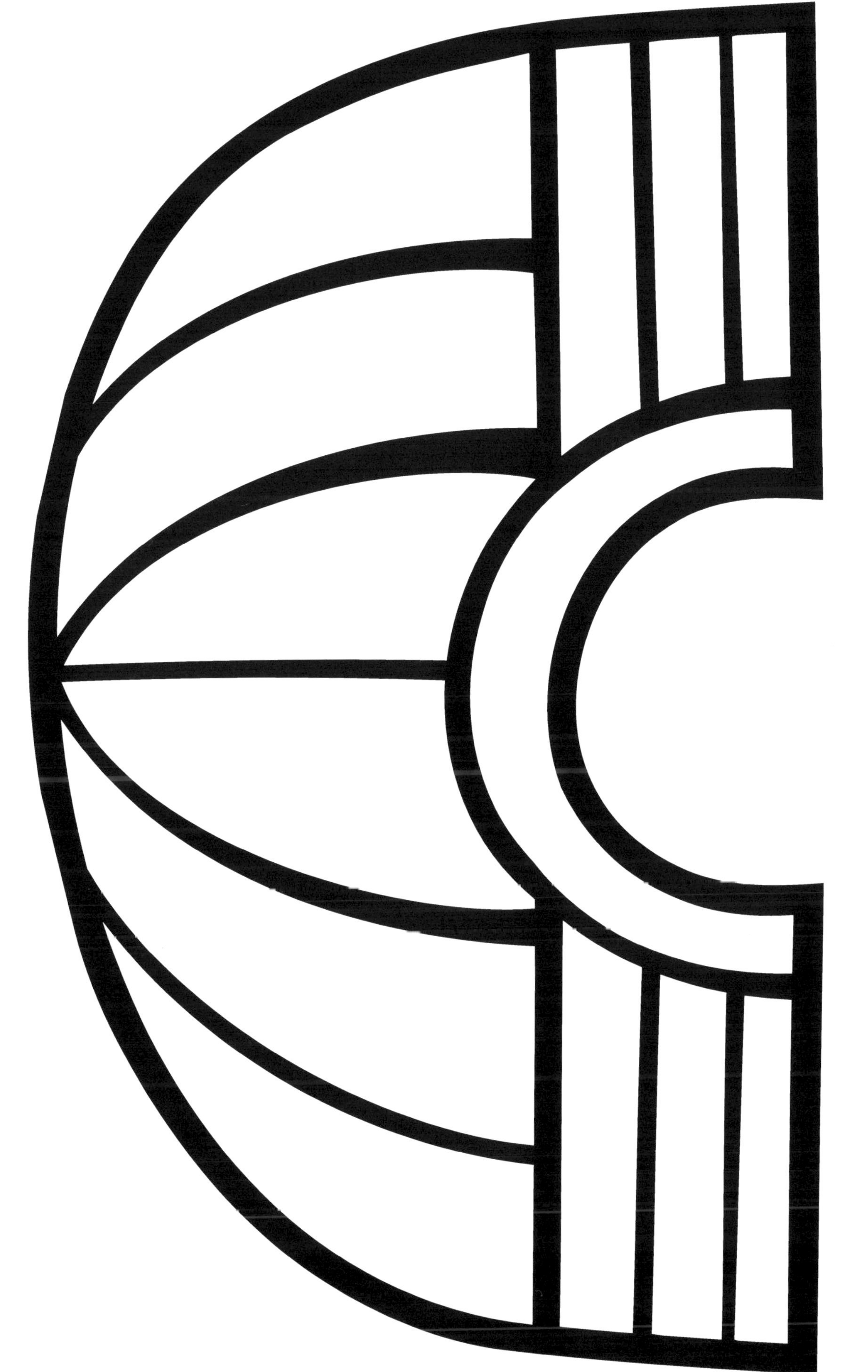

frica Africa Africa Africa

frica Africa Africa Africa

This is a Bleed Through Page If You Are Using a Colouring Marker or Pen!
Find Other Great Titles By searching for Bold Illustrations on Your Favorite Book Retailer
Amazon.Ca | Barnes & Noble (BN.Com) | Books A Million (BAM.Com)

Bold Illustrations
COLORING BOOKS

frica Africa Africa Africa

frica Africa Africa Africa

This is a Bleed Through Page If You Are Using a Colouring Marker or Pen!

Find Other Great Titles By searching for Bold Illustrations on Your Favorite Book Retailer

Amazon.Ca | Barnes & Noble (BN.Com) | Books A Million (BAM.Com)

Bold Illustrations
COLORING BOOKS

frica Africa Africa Africa

Africa Africa Africa Africa

frica Africa Africa Africa

frica Africa Africa Africa

frica Africa Africa Africa

frica Africa Africa Africa

frica Africa Africa Africa

frica Africa Africa Africa

frica Africa Africa Africa

Made in the USA
San Bernardino, CA
18 November 2019

60079121R00058